Collective Consciousness: How to Transcend Mass Consciousness and Become One With the Universe

Dan Desmarques

Published by 22 Lions Bookstore, 2019.

Table of Contents

Copyright Page 1

About the Publisher 3

Introduction 5

What is Mass Consciousness? 7

The Consciousness Reformation 11

The External Influence on Earth 13

The Necessary Quantum Leap 15

The Key to a Higher Consciousness 19

Extraterrestrial Social Systems 23

Extraterrestrial Love and Sexuality 25

The Evolution of Consciousness in a Society 27

Extraterrestrial Consciousness 31

The Metaphysical Assimilation of Reality 33

How Humans Limit Themselves 37

Overcoming the Collective Subconscious 39

The Gate to Freedom 41

The Illusion Created by Money 43

Why Humans Can't Find the Meaning of Life? 45

The Three Dominating Frequencies of Earth 49

How are Humans Controlled by Their Vibrations? 53

Why do People Create Drama? 55

The Relation Between Wealth and Mental Health 57

The Greatest Secret to Wealth and Abundance 59

How to Transcend Mass Consciousness 61

Copyright Page

Collective Consciousness: How to Transcend Mass Consciousness and Become One With the Universe

By Dan Desmarques

Copyright © Dan Desmarques, 2019 (1st Ed.). All Rights Reserved.

Published by 22 Lions Bookstore and Publishing House

About the Publisher

About the 22 Lions Bookstore:

www.22Lions.com

Facebook.com/22Lions

Twitter.com/22lionsbookshop

Instagram.com/22lionsbookshop

Pinterest.com/22lionsbookshop

Introduction

The term cosmic consciousness, or collective consciousness, although widely studied in psychology, and explained by many in the field of spirituality, has never been fully understood and properly clarified at a higher level than the one made possible commonly on Earth. And the reason why, is that these terms are often misinterpreted on a wider scale, for how could we use words such as "cosmic" or "collective" without understanding first awareness from that other standpoint, much wider and more evolved than ours? And how can many claim to understand spirituality without understanding it first from the perspective of higher realms, which transcend our own? Many of such individuals who have attempted that, as I came to know, don't even believe in life on other planets, or have a completely distorted view on how the beings of other galaxies manifest their own consciousness, therefore showing a version of truth which actually manifests their own ideologies. And it is then without a surprise that humanity remains as lost as always, in what regards finding its right path or discarding the wrong ones. For this reason, in this book a clear and linear perspective is shown to you, describing the exact values and mental states that must be acquired by one who wishes to self-evaluate himself on the path towards ascension, for they are interrelated with the same consciousness manifested in realities where the habitants of such worlds are far more evolved than those of Earth. The perspective presented here, although spiritual, is based on the realities presented in many other universes, and therefore explicit in showing you how to find the truth within that will guide you towards a higher evolutionary state, with accuracy, precision, and much faster than what any other method from any other school of knowledge can offer you.

What is Mass Consciousness?

From what I came to understand, within my present amount of perceptions, there is merely a certain proportion of consciousness that is relative to every reality. This means that, in every planet, there are a limited amount of perceptions shared by the collective, living on that particular reality, and which tend to be within a context that both denies inferior and superior patterns to the one experiencing it.

We can better understand this by comparing ourselves with our human past on earth, or even between generations, for it is relatively easy to notice that some values are embraced as more important, while others stay behind, with every transition of time. And although many times it seems to those who stay behind, that there is a certain degradation of choices to embrace, the truth is that there is also a spiritual element that permeates every transition in time and is parallel to any physical demonstration of such transition.

This spiritual element, universal, known as God, God Conscience, Holy Spirit, or merely "The Light", favors and prioritizes a deeper integration between mind, body and soul, along with a more meaningful attribution to our emotions and purpose in life as a collective.

Whenever a transition isn't presented naturally, with fluidity and peacefulness, we will notice a rebellious, anarchic and even violent rupture with old values, in the form of crime, wars and other forms of violence — i.e., immoral acts, and other violations of freewill to a lesser or greater degree.

Death becomes then the ultimate price to pay for a derailing aside from the Divine Truth. And it is because, as a collective, humanity has always sensed this to be a fact, that it has sought to have this Truth protected and embraced by culture, custom and habit.

We can certainly see how this resulted for everyone, for religion has gained a tremendous power out of the needs and fears of the collective, and often used the ignorance of this collective if favor of greedy governments, to fulfill political agendas and even to annihilate the entirety of its followers.

Prophets, such as Jesus, descended to Earth to show exactly this to humanity and were killed, not for religious or spiritual reasons, for the people of his time were more open to religious diversity and worshiping than we would like to believe today, but political reasons.

This division between state and religion, found its greatest conflicts, first with the persecution of the Knights Templar throughout Europe, and then with World War II. In between, we have faced minor but equally significant catastrophes against the free will of its people, with the Inquisition, the persecution of the Gnostics and Cathars, and the creation of political ideologies such as Communism.

Today, the power of religion and government seems to be more unified than ever, thanks to the control both have and share in the fields of science and education. And it is precisely for this reason that humanity has set itself further apart from the Divine Truth, now attributed to these two orders, completely under the authority of those above them, and subjugated to their will, rather than a scientific truth or even the purpose of truly educating the masses. This is why both education and science are organized to favor lobbies, corporations and ideologies that keep this social but tyrannic hierarchy in place.

In between them, we have the media, the secret services and security forces, ensuring that such structure is maintained in order, either through the brainwashing of the masses, the deliberate dumbing down of humanity, or the oppression and arrest of political dissidents.

Interesting how history keeps repeating itself on Earth for thousands of years, no? But taking into consideration that Jesus was trialed in public, rather than eliminated in private under the guise of having committed suicide, and that the Roman Empire was far more liberal on cultural diversity than we are today, especially in big countries like Communist China, where its population represents nearly 20% of the world's population, and it citizens are instigated to spy on each other and foreigners by using mobile applications, we can honestly say that the world of today is far much more oppressive on its people than it ever was before.

COLLECTIVE CONSCIOUSNESS

The hierarchy of humanity is now antinatural, and also Anti-christian, and violates many laws of spirit, which for now show themselves at a deeper level, in the subconscious of the collective, but will, if kept suppressed for long enough, present themselves as the annihilation of the vast masses living of Earth.

The Consciousness Reformation

There's never a transition in time without changes seen at both a spiritual level and physical level, which is, in this last case, created by the collective. In this sense, if one generation favors stagnation during a lifetime, the next will most likely favor its opposite, i.e., a complete detachment from responsibility. And if one generation learns how to go through life by repressing emotions, the next will most likely embrace them uncontrollably.

We can see this transition within one family, from parents to sons and daughters, but it doesn't necessarily mean that one generation is better than another. For we must understand that, within the complexity of our spiritual and cosmic evolution, at the lowest levels of that process, we are still trapped inside the web of religious and cultural values, as well as the system of social organization that we have created for ourselves or learned to accept.

Earth, at this point, is fundamentally an artificial construction made by the minds of many over their experience of survival, and which, for the past centuries, witnessed many devastating wars. And so, the systems we currently have and perceive as being natural, are not natural, but merely the resulting adaptation of centuries of suffering. In other words, we believe in what seems to protect us the most, and we define our mental criteria, and even moral criteria, in such order of priorities.

This is why, whenever governments want to change our order of priorities, or even shift our moral values towards the acceptance of specific political agendas, they will first attack our sense of security, by either allowing or promoting terrorist actions, the spreading of diseases, many of which are created in laboratories, or deliberately threatening our survival with attacks on our bank accounts; all of which are actions that seem to justify themselves with economic, political or cultural reasons, i.e., abstract and intricate motives that nobody is intelligent enough, competent enough, or at the very least, has time enough, to analyze.

Meanwhile, the inappropriateness of such system of beliefs, in its complexities, which interfere in our social order, manifests in our spiritual suffering, our depression, anxieties, and deep need for more from life. And we do, instinctively, try to get more, from our relationships and by forming our own families, to counterbalance all the rest. This is why the concept of love and family is so important for many, and often seen as a basic criteria for survival.

From an emotional standpoint, this behavior makes sense, but realistically speaking, it often lacks trust, honesty, commitment, self-awareness, and many other qualities that few ever realize lacking within themselves. And interestingly enough, it is because of many failed relationships that people eventually decide to visit the office of a therapist, quite often, to find themselves embroiled in a net of never-ending drama. For everything that they sought and believed to be right, suddenly appears wrong; and their identity, often at thirty and forty, or even fifty years of age, is questioned for the first time. Now, imagine this drama being played on a planetary scale, and you are faced with the present condition of Earth.

How can we then understand other live forms, on other planets, with different systems, if we cannot possibly understand our own present condition? For, you see, from an archeological point of view, it seems as if we have been evolving. And meanwhile, this is what archeologists also want to believe. Because, the more we look deeper at our evolution as a species, the more we realize that it is as complex as it is now to identify ourselves as human beings. In other words, there was never a linear evolution, but rather a complex quest for understanding ourselves, that was commonly disrupted with wars and persecution; and this, while our brightest years seem to be attributed to beings, according to reports from around the planet, that came from other planets to help humanity evolve or force it towards such higher stages.

The External Influence on Earth

There have always certainly been beings on Earth, either they were merely prophets, gods, extraterrestrials, or simply enlightened souls, avatars, depending on the approach chosen to describe their actions and living, who walked among us to share with humanity the ultimate truth, or at least how to reach it. Jesus certainly was one among millions of them. But they were many times murdered or discredited before having enough time to share everything they had to offer us, or even before we could understand the fullness and depth of their teachings.

What our messengers were able to give, was reduced to the capacity of the people of their time to understand it. And if we are still puzzled by it, is because two thousand years, or more than that, as in the case of Shiva and others, didn't do much for our development. Only when the teachings of Christ and Shiva become common sense, can we start evolving as a collective, because they did not brought us something of a superior nature, but merely laws in which we must base our conduct to evolve as a species.

Surely, we have denied all that, to pick science as a better and most suitable tool to match our arrogance and egotism as a collective. Science is indeed a more suitable answer to a species that is obsessed with its own brain and the observations of the physical world as a limit to its awareness; and yet, any good scientist who investigates for long enough, ends up dumbfound on the perplexities of how our reality is formed and how much it parallels sacred scripture, if he or she is familiar with any.

The reason why science still gets more credibility than religion is simply due to the fact that humans are at a very low stage of development and need to understand their world through their five senses. They will not be able to understand spirituality until they are able to transcend the world of the senses — physical reality as perceived by the intellect.

The spiritual realms demand an organic approach to be fully comprehended, as opposed to the world of matter, which can be apprehended by our five senses and intellect. And it is natural that evolution is aligned in such away. You can use the same principle to help a child struggling with learning disabilities, for he won't be able to reach a level of complexity and empathy towards the knowledge he has to study, until he first understands its necessity in his personal life and its practical use in the life of others.

Nevertheless, it is now known, due to experiences on DNA, that we have not evolved from monkeys, but are most likely a hybrid between species, and even possibly brought from another planet, which validates the idea of being created on a paradise and then brought to Earth, as the ancient Sumerians wrote. And it is also known that time is a mental construct — past and future don't truly exist except in our mind.

We also know that nothing in the physical world is real, and it is in our brain that things become tangible and touchable. Moreover, the new age philosophers, supported by studies on Quantum Mechanics, have recently introduced us to the idea that we are creators of our own reality, through the patterns of how we think and feel, and even though many spiritualists and magicians have said the same before, through more enigmatic explanations that were not fully comprehended by the masses, still struggling to find something to eat every day.

The Necessary Quantum Leap

It is indeed very difficult to think about spirituality or consciousness, when you need a place to sleep, and food to eat, or when you are afraid that your neighbors might kill you at any moment, or an army may invade your country. It is hard to postulate something further than the "now" when your life can end at any moment. And that is the reason why terror has kept humanity caged for thousands of years, despite the vast amount of information already available.

This does not mean that a quantum leap to a much more evolved reality is not possible at any moment, but that, for that to happen, we would have to change our whole system as a collective; and such event is simply not going to occur anytime soon, despite the many attempts of the most enlightened in asking the masses to look at the truth hidden from them in all areas of human development, such as science (with the works of Nikola Tesla and others, on the topic os free energy), medicine (with the abundance of discoveries on treatments to cure us from deadly diseases, as in the case of Dr. Royal Rife), or mental health (with the research and studies of L. Ron Hubbard and his team).

May you not get confused by the three examples proposed above, for the laboratories of Nikola Tesla and Royal Rife were burned to the ground, after their documents were stolen by private institutions within the government, and L. Ron Hubbard's work, on the field of the mind (which he named Dianetics), became completely discredited thanks to the mass-maniac cult created by an expert in document forgery, narcissist and psychopath, called David Miscavige; and whom, alone, created a tyrannical organization of oppression and extortion called the New Era Church of Scientology, which revised and changed the original works of its founder, and has nothing to do with the original organization, as many former members, who left during or before this takeover, can testify and easily prove.

As a matter of fact, L. Ron Hubbard was a member of Jack Parsons' cult, which, due to the fact that the later worked for NASA, was also strongly influenced by secret extraterrestrial encounters. And that is the basis for Hubbard's understandings of the nature of the mind and how to cure it naturally; a very different approach to what psychiatry is doing today, by attacking the spirit with a vast array of methods and techniques.

No wonder then, that L. Ron Hubbard named Psychiatry the number one enemy of humanity. Psychiatry is, in fact, another tool of the governments for mass control, and is organized in a way that promotes the deterioration and destruction of free will in an individual, a community, a country or even a whole planet. And interestingly enough, many psychiatrists have admitted exactly this, when stating that their methods of analysis and practices are completely arbitrary and without any medical foundation. Despite this, and the complete lack of interest of the masses on this topic, there are many evidences of their statements on camera and in well-made documentaries.

Since then, and until now, many documents publicly released by the CIA and the FBI, among other governmental institutions from around the globe, testify that many visitors from other constellations continue to come to Earth in their spaceships, to share amazing technology and knowledge with us. And yet, it will all continue being suppressed by private groups into their own interests, and towards specific goals, because of how Earth is politically structured. The story of Valiant Thor is probably one of the most sad and representative of the greed of humanity, for his knowledge was refused to protect corporative interests.

Everything threatening the system, as it is found today, namely, in what regards religious organizations and beliefs, governments as we see them, healthcare and medicine, the pharmaceutical industry, and the concept of nation as we understand it, or hierarchy as we know it, is still completely ignored when offered by such visitors, and while the entire focus of our interactions with them permeates only and above wall, weaponry and combat technology. We are still stuck on an ideology of fear, and we will continue to be, while evolving with our technology in such direction — self-destruction. This, until such system of beliefs is disrupted with a major war that makes us, again, question ourselves and our values as a whole.

COLLECTIVE CONSCIOUSNESS

What a shame that is, for you cannot even image what it would be like, if suddenly, we were allowed to move forward in time, by ten thousand years or much more. That's how far stuck in primitive systems and ways of living we still are as a collective, and despite the vast amount of information already at our disposal. Could it then be difficult to imagine this possibility on another planet? For it is not only difficult to imagine it, but necessary, as it is already a reality.

The Key to a Higher Consciousness

Many well intentioned people believe that a rise on the levels of empathy can change everything, and that would indeed be the key to a higher consciousness. This is what extraterrestrials have been expecting from us, more than anything else, for it would justify a more permanent interference of their higher values on Earth to elevate ours and improve our living standards. But I am not so optimistic in what regards to that, and therefore, I share the same preoccupation of our visitors, whom constantly watch over us, just in case we decide to begin a great war against ourselves.

You see, empathy will not do much for humanity unless a person can do more than praying, and that's taking action, in any direction, either to improve oneself, help others, or improve the state of the planet. But most people are in such an apathetic state of consciousness, that they can only repeat "not my problem" or "I can't do it alone" or even "I can't change anything". All of these thoughts come from the idea of individualism, or distorted selfishness — The idea that we can't form a group based on higher ideologies, or that those can only be created by some, enlightened, or with special qualifications. In many cases, sitting still and ignoring reality, is seen as the ultimate goal, and thought of as being mediation for common good. Few people understand that meditation is a very low level of mental training, far below many others, even though necessary, when one is completely lost in self-destructive and irrational thoughts or intends to give a positive contribution to the collective subconscious.

The irrational laws of the planet can't be disrupted unless broken. And for that to happen, one has to interfere within that which he also hates. Interesting how we can't escape the laws of the planet, isn't? And yet, many would say that this is being negative, and that being positive consists in being a big child pretending that evil and problems don't exist, that we will all be fine if we believe that everything is already good as it is, and perfect, without the need for any interference.

Such people are actually a total disgrace for what good journalism represents or the purpose of scientific research, for they deny facts and allow their mind to be violated, just to avoid confrontation with reality. They sink deeper into their subconscious, and in doing so, to lower levels of consciousness. And if they meditate, they are merely wasting their time and driving themselves crazy. For when you meditate to escape reality, you are using meditation to destroy the instincts and emotional web within you that make you human, and descending into the lowest chakras, while blocking those above the one where you find yourself in, with suppressed pain, suppressed resentment and suppressed anger. That, is also the formula for depression and a permanent apathy.

It is actually interesting, how such people end up finding comfort on other lunatics like them. Because, you see, the new age gurus, are nearly all wrong, when they claim that an ascension will go through all problems and make them vanish, as if by ignoring a problem, it will simply disappear. That's a human belief indeed, that everyone in spiritual circles love. It's the "If I don't think about it, it's not real." But such principle denies the following one, requiring an action on the opposite direction — I.e., that you need to work towards change for changes to occur. And this is why so many extraterrestrials, obviously frustrated, visit us for so many thousands of years — they want us to work towards those changes, and not just look mesmerized at them, as we often do with our popstars and fireworks in the sky.

Humans are very well-controlled by long lasting ideologies that make them stupid, incapable of learning from that which they admire. And so, they tend to evolve on a horizontal level, rather than vertical. Humans always embrace that which makes them more of what they already are. And this is why books on intelligence and competition, or war, sell so well. This is also why drugs sell even more. And yet, this is also why books that lead to enlightenment are typically ignored and rejected by the masses.

Yes, you read it correctly. Most books promoting enlightenment are not truly offering it. Because the type of spirituality that people seek and promote, is often permeated by a horizontal perspective, focused on acceptance, resignation and stagnation. Hardly, anyone who reads spiritual books, will want to read about responsibility, actions and postulates. And that's the basis of true spirituality.

COLLECTIVE CONSCIOUSNESS

But you find it most commonly on books about business and money. Isn't this ironic? We find more about spirituality on topics related to the material world and a control of such world, through independent acts and attitudes, such as entrepreneurship. And I do believe, after a long experience with both sides of society, that such individuals — business founders, understand much better any spiritual topic and can have a more profound religious conversation, than anyone else who can't understand how money is made.

Now, this puts the concept of "popular books" and "best seller" under a completely new light, isn't it? For what the masses consider good or great, is nothing more than a reinforcement of their own present state. Few are those who will love that which changes them to an upper stage.

Extraterrestrial Social Systems

Other beings also have a social system, a set of values, goals, and emotions, that can manifest more predominantly in one spectrum than others. There is no such thing as a single evolutionary pattern, as evolution can play itself in many directions. There is indeed a singularity of manifestations, meaning that they all show a certain set of coincidences within a vast array of representations of life, as what we see in the animal kingdom, and that includes empathic manifestations at various degrees, a synergy of goals, a shared or common collective consciousness, as we have on Earth, and albeit unaware of it, and also a certain paradigm moving them collectively towards evolution.

This does not mean, however, that evolution is balanced at all levels, or that such thing even exists as we perceive it. But it means that planetary beings evolve collectively within a certain amount of values and within certain behavior patterns. For this reason, it is not a coincidence that humans, as many other races, have evolved differently, when manifesting themselves in different planets, where they have or not the freedom to do so. But I will explain it more clearly: When such freedom exists, humans may evolve collectively towards certain interests, depending on how they choose to organize themselves; it depends on who is leading the collective and how such collective reacts to it. In other cases, the collective is manifesting the lead of its rulers as a singularity. And yet, both situations manifest somehow, and to a certain degree, for people only tolerate that which they are able to tolerate; i.e., leaders always manifest within a certain level of consciousness and are maintained by that same level, until it shifts. This is the same principle behind the reason why the French couldn't accept monarchy but the Chinese do accept totalitarian and much worse hierarchical systems of domain over them, such as with the case with communism.

Now, by values, I want to explain you that, whenever technology prevails over others things, like empathy, you may see a collective race moving fiercely towards military control and planetary acquisitions. Such is the predominante, although not exclusive, case of the many draconian races.

Insectoid humanoids, on the other hand, manifest a more predominant collective consciousness as their priority. And it doesn't mean that they don't have an individuality of their own or technological development, but rather that such things tend to follow the priority put on the collective consciousness. What I mean by that, is that their emotions are fulfilled by the collective; nobody ever feels lonely, and love is such a clear thing for them, that relationships occur spontaneously, without the need to think over them, as humans typically do on Earth, many times by filtering their own partners with reasoning.

When two Insectoid humanoids fall in love, it occurs first at a vibrational level and then the communication is perceived telepathically, and followed accordingly, without the need to think if it's suitable or not for such two beings to be together. In fact, the only reason why humans do that, is because their system and survival depends on the cooperation within the duality found in a couple. And yet, we find today its opposite, a big and global rupture with old patterns, with people gladly having sex with strangers they meet in bars and clubs, as if that was the most natural thing to do or even resembling postmodernism. It's not, and it actually represents the opposite of a relationship based on survival, a setback on spiritual evolution — these individuals are merely having sexual pleasure and not truly building a family or feeling love. They are, if anything, denying themselves love with the act; and that's why, in the long run, such behaviors of promiscuity have consequences on the soul, degrading the being towards lower levels of frequency, where lack of self-love is also manifested, and neurosis is developed.

Such trend has serious consequences on humanity as a whole too, and represents a division within society rather than a gradual transition, for the offspring of such people often lack the basic empathic skills for survival within a state of collective consciousness. In other words, promiscuity breeds narcissists. And that is why it is and has always been considered a sin, for it lowers the vibrational level between generations, breaking the spirit and opening the mind to demonic possession.

Extraterrestrial Love and Sexuality

Still in what regards the topic of sexuality, I was once asked by Freemasons with more than sixty years of study on this topic, if on alien planets there is polyamory, and they were disappointed when I told them that it isn't common, for they have been led to believe, by many ignorant spiritual leaders, the exact opposite.

In the very few cases in which a being has multiple lovers, they usually all represent different roles, and are always at an inferior state when compared to the predominant male, even though, for such beings, there is no such thing as equality, or the concept of inferiority, not as humans perceive the terms, but rather a differentiation of roles based on biological needs and tendencies. The very fact that humans need equality is what proves them incapable of healthy polyamorous relationships.

Such alien realities would obviously be very shocking to witness when contrasted with the values presented on Earth, but it is the equivalent to having one dominating male within a collective of females, each one having a different role in the family, as in one being responsible for his sexuality, another for the food in the house, and another one taking care of tasks that we often consider a hobby or mere entertainment. Furthermore, in these situations, the relationship among everyone is solidified on happiness and commitment, rather than sex. In fact, the more sexual a species is, the less likely polyamory is to be found. For the principles that justify polyamory cannot be understood by a species deeply rooted on its sexual needs for validation at a personal and social level.

The law that governs sexuality at a cosmic level is in accordance with sacred geometry, as the force that pulls one element towards another, denies the transition to the formation of the third element. And that third element, for the human species, comes in the form of offspring. Whenever an individual isn't spiritually evolved enough, he or she will simply not love children, not want children, and actually tend to have an averse reaction towards children. And we would, necessarily, have to be able to love the children of others, before we could understand polyamory. And as a collective, the human race is still very far from that stage.

Therefore, those who consider themselves polyamorous, are actually narcissists, and love nobody, not even themselves, and justify lustful desires with polyamory, simply because that is the only way they have of securing their sexual partners' presence in their life and justifying their behavior with a term that makes them look anything but psychotic; i.e., they lie to one another for practical and selfish reasons.

Spirituality is not an option for such souls, and they are typically atheists or followers of a distorted view of religion, most likely resembling demonology, and the cult of the ego, for it worships what they can't have — self-love. And it is important to mention that orgasm without self-love is a very dangerous ritual.

Marriage can be seen as a universal tendency, even though not contractual as we typically have on Earth. Marriage, at a higher spiritual level, is the relation that one being has with another, with complete honesty and trust, as if that other individual was an extension of himself or herself. And only in such cases, can we verify a predominance of equality between genders.

It is worth mentioning as well that, due to their attitude of total openness towards emotions and love, Insectoid Humanoids do not experience mental illnesses as humans do. They tend to put a higher value on love and connections between them, and such relations are always based on Divine Love, which they telepathically and organically feel within their bodies as real.

Now imagine this: How would you feel, if you loved everyone around you? Would you feel as if your identity was being somehow denied? Probably! That reaction would be normal for an Earthly being. But that's also what I mean by different races having different set of values and social priorities.

The Evolution of Consciousness in a Society

Different evolutionary states, open the mind to different perceptions of the physical world, which humans are simply not evolved enough yet to comprehend. Most things, which are normal in many other planets, such as telepathic communication, horribly scare a lot of people on Earth — they can't live with the idea that someone can simply read their mind. And I don't need to tell you that I lose all my friends and relationships once they perceive me doing it.

Fortunately for me, however, as most people don't believe and don't want to believe in this possibility, they also can't consider me a threat to them; not unless they want to lie to me. For in this case, they end up terribly frustrated, and attempt to manipulate me and insult me in many ways. This, because the vast majority of the humans on Earth are just too selfish and jealous to understand love, much less life. Rather than changing with my presence, which they can't, due to the implications they can't handle (and interestingly enough, all of which related to the system that controls them, i.e., educational values, cultural beliefs, and the paradigms of their coworkers they expose themselves to on a daily basis), they attempt to bring me down to their level, in order to be able to love me from their evolutionary level; and that doesn't mean that, because I can see it, I can control it, for I always end up exhausting myself in the process — humans don't change by themselves, but only and always as a collective. Individual change, even if strongly forced by the emotion of love, is always too scary for anyone to justify a departure from the old spiritual self. Most people rather suffer in their collective self instead of rejoicing on their individual self. And that pretty much resumes the dramas of people's life on Earth.

Many humans would say that such relationships are not based on love, but I would have to disagree on this rather ignorant and simplistic observation of reality. That's not an accurate analysis, when perceived from a wider angle, more empathic too, for you can't blame a tiger for eating the human who feeds him, or realistically assume that you can find a non-human-eating tiger.

Likewise, and for the exact same reasons, many relationships, formed under practical motives, such as financial needs and social validation, can last, especially, if both individuals are within a similar frame of reference. That, however, won't ever occur when one is much more evolved and possesses superhuman capacities, such as telepathy.

I did notice a higher sexual fulfillment, as well as desire, in the feline races; and also a sense of independence most strongly manifested in these. And yet, their level of aggression and wild lifestyle is incompatible with most Earthly humans, who can't imagine themselves living on a planet where nature is a priority; and so, their high sexual drive is also perfectly compatible with their highly energetic lifestyle.

Humanoid felines literally adopted the jungle as their home and love their planet exactly as it is. These patterns, for humanity of Earth, obsessed with physical structures, wouldn't seem natural. Humans feel more comfortable in building block structures, composed by physical order, and in being placed in a box, which they call home. That's why humans love their cities, and that's why there's a tendency for cities to grow while villages become isolated ghost towns.

Harmony with nature is not something that humans can enjoy or feel comfortable with, because it makes them feel out of control, out of their habitat. And so, we can say that humans don't deserve Earth, as much as Earth is not for them. Humans have been left on Earth as a slave race, but did a horrible job with the planet. And so, this planet is being destroyed because of the selfish mentality that humans have; and this behavior is currently very destructive.

The removal of humans from Earth, is a Divine wish, but not related to their salvation, as many christians would think. Surely, we can believe that, if a few are removed into a better habitat. It's a way of looking at it. But, nonetheless, this is also a necessary action to save the planet and let it prosper for another race that will most surely appreciate it.

COLLECTIVE CONSCIOUSNESS

Humans need to be placed on a paradise, i.e., a planet that suits their vibratory nature better, and where they will do no destruction — a better asylum for their souls, to develop in harmony, rather than in permanent conflict with the outside world, and among themselves, for resources and security. And for these reasons, it wouldn't make any sense if all had that same chance and fate.

Extraterrestrial Consciousness

The most impressive realization for me, and from all my experiences with different alien races, has to do with the concept of awareness, as most beings perceive reality from a very different angle, wider, most-likely, related to a natural evolution that guided them there, to that state of complete balance. It impressed me deeply, the deep and almost complete relation some beings have with their technology, not as a replacement for their capacities, as we see happening on Earth, but rather a complement to them and their societies, their lifestyle, and this, by creating a perfect correlation between their telepathic use, emotions and the material world — which is operated by vibrations controlled remotely with their thoughts and emotions.

Another huge realization for me, is related to the concept of love, and how it is perceived at the highest levels, and how different it is from the way humans process it.

Many times these visions trespass what I am capable of handling when conscious, and so when I wake up afterwards, I feel somehow confused, while trying to adjust myself and my human mind, to what I learned during sleep or under a meditative state. But love, was certainly a big lesson for me, one of the biggest I ever experienced, especially because I felt it as one of them, in one of my past lives.

I have never felt love in such a way with my human body. It felt more organic and honest too. Because, you see, to love with your mind and heart in complete truth, is very different of having such emotion filtered by your beliefs and perception of reality; it is also more real and complete. And it only feels scary for many humans to experience this, because of the mental implications it has — to surrender to our emotions and to love and to give ourselves to someone else entirely and for life.

The lack of trust humans have on their own nature, leads them to actually do the opposite, when loving gradually or never entirely. This is also why many humans have never fully enjoyed their sexuality, no matter how many partners they may have had. For they don't know what is to enjoy sex organically, and mentally, and not just purely physically or focused on their genitals.

My visions of my past lives on other planets have changed me so much, that, just as any other traveler that wonders the world, getting all of its priceless insights, I gradually, but inevitably, started using my renewed perspective on life and evolution in my books and in everything I write. That's why they feel so real for so many people, including those who have read plenty others on the same topics; it is because my work is indeed more real, based on what I've experienced on many other planets, living in other bodies and feeling life differently, as many different extraterrestrial races.

These memories, when they returned to me, answered so many questions, that I actually started using that perspective in my writings to explain a huge variety of topics, and to make them more clear, namely, ancient religious topics, such as alchemy or spiritual evolution through prayer, or the system of chakras. But I also don't know if it's because I write books on spirituality, that I am constantly fed with those visions and memories, as many times, I am receiving information from other sources and not only my subconscious mind.

I was, nevertheless, certainly chosen to come here and to be in communication with the extraterrestrial beings from many other planets and galaxies. And from what I came to understand, it is because I am a galactic soldier, not in the sense of what is perceived on Earth, reason why the fortunetellers that were able to see this about me couldn't understand their own visions or explain them properly to me, but a different concept of soldier.

Moreover, many fortunetellers I encountered don't believe in extraterrestrials, even though they claim to believe. Most people stupidly believe that this is a concept too far from their world, so they can't even perceive the possibility of having one, in front of them, in a human body.

The Metaphysical Assimilation of Reality

It's really interesting to see how people deny what they claim to believe and throw away all of their ideas on reincarnation and extraterrestrials whenever having to confront the truth, just because they can't handle it. In other words, people want to believe that everything is outside of them, and not within them or much less in front of them.

The concept of interplanetary soldier, however, has a specific meaning that is not real to Earthlings, and so, is difficult for me to put it here in words. Such being is not a militar on the horrific sense of the word, nor is he a jedi, as fiction movies portray. He is, as many travelers from other galaxies, an explorer — vulnerable to the differences among planetary manifestations, and yet, the most suitable to adapt to them.

Surely, intelligence, may not manifest as it is perceived on Earth; this type of intelligence, as explained before, comes from the spirit — it is the capacity to interact emotionally and telepathically with the world around one, and easily, through empathy, by feeling such world. Again, it is a form of spiritual adaption, and obviously, can confuse many that possess the same abilities, as they often tend to confuse themselves with the world around them, and, in doing so, feel inferior when compared to such world, incapable of coping with the levels of aggression and the psychological demands around them.

This is why a spiritual connection to higher realms is relevant here, as such souls are constantly receiving commands from above, which at the beginning they assume as coming from God, and only later understand better, first with dreams, then visions, and finally memories of past lives on other planets.

It is only at this stage, when the individual completely accepts his eternal identity as an intergalactic soldier, that he is able to open the final gate of his mind, and receive information on command. And this is my case now, as I can easily channel the answer to all my questions from such realities. And yet, they come with a purpose, as I must put them in books to share them with the human race.

My consciousness is relative to my work on Earth, so I can't possibly be arrogant about my job, as it comes as a service, not only to humans, but the whole cosmic consciousness. If anything, I rather keep my human identity private, to continue enjoying the benefits of experiencing a human life.

This would end forever if I was surrounded by a group of people that knew who I was, and my public identity was forever shattered as either a lunatic, a schizophrenic, a conspiracy theorist or an avatar, an indigo or an angel.

I have been called all these things, because humans always need to see reality from their own personal standpoint and spiritual evolutionary level. And I don't believe I would ever find people seeing me beyond these terms, and as I really am, for they would have to be more evolved than the Earthly vibratory state to be able to see so well.

It is easy for me to prove that I am not a lunatic. I have done it countless times with psychologists, psychiatrists and many religious organizations. It's also easy for me to prove that I am an avatar. I have done it several times with Freemasons and Rosicrucians. But to make random people believe that I am not crazy but an avatar, that's another story; because, as I mentioned previously, the vast majority of the people on Earth, is not ready for what they claim to believe.

In other words, I have not met anyone on Earth that claims to believe in Extraterrestrials or Reincarnation and wants to confront me, or even test me. They are afraid of the truth. So, they are actually the crazy ones, for claiming to believe things they don't. The large majority of the freemasons, rosicrucians, and scientologists, are hypocrites, liars, unconscious of their own very low level of spiritual evolution, and too arrogant for the little they know and can accept. And yet, I have not found groups that possess more knowledge than these three, knowledge that can help humanity evolve to what I call the basic stage of awakening.

COLLECTIVE CONSCIOUSNESS

What many call enlightenment is really just primary school on an evolutionary and cosmic scale. Humans are merely learning how to read, when studying consciousness. But the vast majority is not even within this school themselves, for they are entertaining themselves with foolishness like little children in kindergarten.

How Humans Limit Themselves

I learn so much from my visions, memories and dreams, that I am now understanding better the state of planet Earth. In fact, taking into consideration that for many years I felt that I couldn't understand humans, and even contemplated the possibly of being retarded, nothing of what I know now surprises me in what regards my own background. For only a very conscious being would even consider his own retardation when compared to a whole species, and learn to evolve towards matching his communication patterns and value system with the world around him. I have never seen a human doing this, even in what regards either his own ignorance or arrogance.

Still regarding this topic, I must say, if it helps you in your own life, that the greatest lesson I ever learned during my journey on Earth, is that humans are indeed blocked by themselves — their own delusional belief on reality — and possibly due to the many lifetimes of being trapped inside the same planet.

It is indeed interesting how so many theories that promote the exclusive use of the brain over other parts of the body, have been and continue being promoted all over the planet, because that's exactly where the trap lays, i.e., in methods that make humans more rational, more visual, more exclusive to their thoughts and physical senses, and less intuitive, less aware of their spiritual nature.

Humans, today, process absolutely everything within their brain, including love. And so, the brain ends up acting as a trap for the identity, justifying the emotions captured by the heart, and the thoughts found in the mind. Except that Earthlings don't know that their thoughts are often captured from others, and their emotions too, which makes it paradoxically dramatic and funny to witness, as it is as if people were being played around completely unaware of it, and while thinking that they have an identity of their own. Many even look at me perplexed, when I ask them: Do you think your thoughts or your thoughts think you?

People, typically, don't even know the difference. Many don't even believe they can control their own thoughts, much less create them. In other words, they are completely unaware to the fact that they are constantly absorbing the thoughts of others, and processing their own by default, not knowing the difference between both, not even knowing how their stupidity affects the stupidity of others. Basically, human consciousness, nowadays, is just a very big trashcan. And that's why humans suffer with so many mental illnesses.

Surely, this scenario becomes worse, when they can't even tell how ghosts interfere with their thoughts and emotions, but that's another new level to debate, not relevant to what this book intends to show you. In other words, and to resume what was said above, the brain creates excuses for what people feel and see but can't understand, and does it automatically. People are constantly projecting justifications, to deny themselves their state of craziness, and that's why they love mass hysteria, in the form of "belief-trends". They will say things like "you made me mad", or "I can't handle people like that", or "they made me do it", or "men this and women that", while completely unaware, during the whole time, that they have been fabricating excuses for what they would have end up doing anyway; for they can't have any control over themselves, as much as they have no control over their thoughts.

That's what makes everyone so predictable too. You know, it's like when people visit a fortuneteller and believe what she says, or the opposite, when they say: "I don't believe any of that". One way or another, they are operating by default, totally blind to their lack of causation over their fate.

In the first case, they are assuming that their fate is built, which it is, especially if self-discipline and awareness are denied; and in the second case, they are denying all that, plus the idea that fate exists, which is the same as being completely in the dark, not knowing you can hit the things around you. The first group knows they are blind and does nothing about it, while the second group does not do anything about it while denying they are even blind.

Overcoming the Collective Subconscious

The subconscious mind of the majority is just the first step of this whole mechanism, because, actually, if people keep operating within their brain, they will always, truly always, get trapped by the outside world, a world which, nevertheless, they keep imposing on themselves. But how could humans do otherwise, if they were never trained or taught to act differently, and never saw anyone else doing things differently?

There's just not even sufficient knowledge on Earth to show humanity that humans are not mental creatures, but emotional and vibrational beings. And until this happens, until it is shown to the masses, they won't start processing their reality with their higher senses, and evolving towards what they can perceive with those.

In fact, as some people, to whom I have shown how to do this, have told me, it's extremely scary to make such evolutionary jump from the standpoint where humanity is today. And why it is so scary? Because, suddenly, you realize that some people whom you considered your best friends, are either psychotic or possessed by demons. You may also realize you have been living your whole life under completely wrong beliefs, which forces you now to change towards a new path, if you really want to be your true self — and that's scary, because it represents the unknown, and yet, an unknown where you feel completely alone, which just makes it worse. It's like being put in paradise by yourself with nobody else to share it with.

You would most likely want to return to hell just to have some company. And well, that's what Earth is — the hell of the most elevated souls, and also the heaven of the most inferior.

As I usually say to people who can't understand me, and insist on saying that I am crazy and their reality is perfect, "the fact that someone who doesn't like to read, thinks that an author of more than four hundred books, member of many religious organizations and business owner, former college lecturer, and business consultant, is crazy, says more about the one claiming it and believing it, than it says about the person being labeled"; "and there must be something terribly wrong with how your brain functions, as well as your mental health, if you can't feel angry when insulted by your friends, or outraged when fooled by society, if you want to believe that your government is interested in your own good, and if you believe that human beings are normal creatures, and not just completely insane and very ignorant in vast numbers."

Awakening to a world where most people are completely out of their mind, is like awakening to a world full of zombies and realize you are totally alone, fighting for your own survival. It's very scary and demands lots of courage. It's not for a common individual. Therefore, most people actually deny the possibility of evolving spirituality.

Surely, many will tell you that such is not true, because they meditate and go to yoga classes, and follow a guru. And to these I must say that a head massage is not the same as a sexual orgasm and shouldn't be compared to one. You are not evolving until you truly loose track of who you were and become someone new — a higher and bigger version of yourself, with more perceptions, more awareness, and a more effective response over the mechanisms of life, with an equal capacity to feel anger as much as to feel love in a more profound and organic state.

The extreme of what I just said is seen in reincarnation, with the death of a personality and the discarding of its body, to awake in a new one, in a new culture, with a complete new set of rules and values.

At an even more extreme state, we find the reincarnation on new planets, surely not suitable to the many fragile souls on Earth, that can't even handle their own life, their own truths, much less deeper emotions, as the ones many extraterrestrials experience as a norm.

The Gate to Freedom

The way out of the asylum found on Earth, is indeed, as many philosophers and teachers of the past have said, within.

I never understood how the way out is within, not fully, until my dreams of past lives on other alien bodies have shown me this through direct experience. Such experiences, allowed me to feel and see how other beings live their life and perceive it. And so, the answer is actually simpler than I ever imagined, because it doesn't imply complicated meditation procedures or anything similar to that. We do require a certain training, that is not "normal" to Earth right now, but it consists on living more by the spirit and the heart, and less by the head.

Sure, this is a complex topic, when we can't understand our emotions or visions, and much less control them. But that's what I noticed about other beings the most — they live by the heart, and they can't even conceptualize life differently. And although it seems like a joyful hippie version of reality, the funny thing is that, once moral and honesty and compassion and empathy are added to this mixture, everything else flows well into the common paradigm of the whole civilization, and you will feel high on joy the entire time. And so, even though in each planet the beings organize themselves differently and within different set of social values, they are all happy; or at least not feeling "forced" into a life that feels "unnatural to them", as humans experience theirs.

Along this line, it's interesting to see the reactions of the people I encounter, when I tell them that I don't need to work but do it for pleasure. It's like telling them that I come from another planet. They react in the same way, with disbelief, distrust, and in many cases, even fear.

The most common reaction is to think that I lie, or that I do something illegal I can't talk about. Even when I explain them that my businesses and books all work and sell by themselves, while I sleep, they still can't understand this.

Somehow, humans have forgotten how life works. And that's why, even though they are obsessed with money, they can't even perceive how it is being created for centuries, since it was invented. I don't think most people even believe anymore that money is an invention of their own. And that's how very stupid humanity is right now, constantly forgetting what it creates for itself. Humans are literally victims of their own imbecility for millions of years.

The Illusion Created by Money

There is no concept of "need to work" or "money" in other planetary systems, although value is presented in contributions to the energy that is absorbed and shared by the community as a whole. In other words, roles are perfectly accepted for they feel meaningful. And while in some cases, I saw no clear difference between males and females, more often than not, I did saw a clear difference. And the same applies to hierarchies, which tend to be inexistent, due to the fact that most extraterrestrial races believe in the concept of common good and freedom, i.e., the need to explore their own will and creative desires, their own life as a collective, rather than sacrificing their time to an idea.

Most extraterrestrials have evolved far beyond that — which is actually just another human conceptualization for the enslavement of themselves — and have their societies automatized, and working for them, to support their lifestyle, which is actually not as luxurious as we, humans, in our greed, tend to desire.

Having a family and exploring knowledge as a collective in the galaxy is a priority for the majority of the human races. And if you wish to compare it with a similar situation on planet Earth right now, simply imagine yourself having full-time vacations with your family and reading for fun the whole time about a vast variety of topics. If you can't imagine this, or don't desire it, you are simply not evolved enough to leave this planet. It's as simple as that.

It feels normal to me to be able to work when I want, to feel pleasure in my work, and to live where I want, and to travel the whole planet when I want, and I don't understand why this is so strange for human beings, why it feels so unnatural and unreal to them.

At the current stage of things on Earth, with this battle of who is better, men or women, me or you, them or us, these ideologies can even be confusing or offensive to many. And yet, in most planets, genders are differentiated not by rules, but by social and organic meanings. Each gender feels perfectly well adjusted in fulfilling its biological role, and see as ridiculous the act of forcing oneself against his own instincts and nature. But again, the whole structure is so well organized, that it feels natural even by looking at the whole system of the planet. And this is another thing I learned about Earth: most people are conditioned by a chaotic system of values, still trying to adjust itself from past centuries; and so, we end up in endless debates about what should or should not be done, permitted, legalized or made illegal, rather than seeing who we really are. Because, well, we don't know who we really are as humans.

Why Humans Can't Find the Meaning of Life?

Humans don't know what to do with their existence, because, basically, they don't know who they are as an organism, or what promotes their survival the most as a collective consciousness. But that's the battle between "brain" and "nature" that humans insist on having and that delays their natural spiritual progress. That's also what makes them crazy as a collective.

I realized this by comparing the information obtained with the people around me and what they say, when they behave as if I was wrong for enjoying life, or not working when I feel like reading a book. They do not truly understand the meaning of life, and judge me based on a system they know nothing about. But this is what leads me to think that the vast majority of the souls on Earth have been here for so many thousands of years, that they can't even perceive anything else beyond these constructs. Most of what I see, do and tell them, scares them up to a state of terror.

In fact, it doesn't take me long to realize, by looking at certain paradigms and values, where most people are. And here's the funny part of what I realize when observing and comparing the stage of Earth with the neighbors in the cosmos: Most humans are not even here; they are stuck in the 50s and the 60s, or even before that. Most people in their 30s are still stuck in paradigms of their past life.

So, in truth, before acknowledging that humans need to evolve as a species to higher stages of consciousness, in order to embrace a more fulfilling existence, we need to recognize the global mental catastrophe of billions and billions of souls, trapped in traumas of past life existences, most of which are indeed too painful to even remember. This, when they're not trapped in a childlike and infantile mindset. For there is also the case of a vast amount of people who did not truly evolved past their childhood, as any tests in modern psychology can show you.

We have been too cruel to one another, many times in the name of good, and those atrocities remain among us, commanding our instincts before our emotions and decisions, controlling our mind and mastering over it. Humans are truly all crazy on this Earth, and it's amazing how the world organizes itself and functions despite that. Somehow, this big asylum for the mentally and spiritually ill, was made a colony for souls that are limited by their own condition, and feels normal to these, who cannot see themselves in what I just described.

How humans made themselves insane before, is a topic for another book. But I can tell you in advance that insanity is promoted due to a violation of spiritual laws and criminal acts, against oneself and others. And so, we can't deny that humans are mental ill, as much as they are paying the price for criminal acts of the past.

In other words, if you can gather the people currently held in prisons and psychiatric hospitals, and put them all together on Mars, you will start seeing this planet in the same manner as Extraterrestrials see Earth, and then understand them better.

Like in other realms, this planet also has laws that can be seen in our interactions; but let us remember what was said previously, as most people are not aware of why they feel and think the way they do, and try to justify such mechanisms to deny consciousness; and so, the less spiritual they are, the more they do these things, the more self-absorbed they are, reason why atheists, as well as agnostics, tend to be extremely neurotic and psychotic for these same reasons.

There's no better way to end this chapter than to explain it with a practical example that occurred to me, when I tried to show a friend how she creates her own dramas, by repeating relationship after relationship with men that just want to have sex with her and nothing else, and despite doing the same for years, with dozens of men. I said to her:

— "You are projecting your expectations on others, because you are unable to accept your delusional expectations on yourself, and in doing so, process your true self-worth, rather than the idea that you are superior to others because your parents and closest friends make you believe that."

She felt offended and, in an attempt to insult me, replied back:

— "No, I am not; you are the one who projects your expectations on others and is confused."

COLLECTIVE CONSCIOUSNESS

I could only laugh at the situation. For there's really no way you will ever convince a fool of his foolishness. And that resumes the insane state of humanity.

This story can also help you in understanding why most extraterrestrial races believe that showing themselves to humans and explain their knowledge to humanity is a complete waste of time and efforts. The possibility of that ever resulting in a positive outcome is scarce. And along this explanation, you can also understand why only a few humans would ever deserve being rescued from complete annihilation.

The Three Dominating Frequencies of Earth

I have struggled during my entire life, with my earthly family, my classmates, coworkers, and now, in present time, and at nearly forty years of age, with basically everyone I encounter around the world, trying to understand why I am so hated, so attacked, with any kind of excuses and wherever I go, for no apparent reason, except mental fabrications of whoever can't handle my presence.

In countries where the predominant energy level is very low, such as Portugal, China, The Phillipines, Indonesia, Turkey, Lithuania, and Spain, but also some parts of the United States, such as Florida, I found myself being insulted and stared the whole time, by complete strangers. They are, nonetheless, a majority, and so it is very hard to explain, to the common mortal, how is this even possible. And yet, despite these events, I have noticed that those who experienced them with me also cannot believe their own eyes. Yes, they see it, and they can't believe it. They go into denial.

In their head, they start fabricating excuses for what has occurred, and that can't possibly be explained by any logical reason. In fact, many of such acquaintances start avoiding me, because the experiences I have, even if I am the victim, scare them.

Now, the question is, why should I, as the victim, scare others? Why aren't people scared for what this shows in what regards the current state of humanity on Earth? Well, because, indeed, this proves, without a doubt, that humans are extremely mentally ill, and to realize that, one would have to acknowledge his own insanity and responsibility in moving out of it, alone, and also expect to battle a whole army of crazies surrounding him in his daily life; and most people are too scared of doing that, because they seek the exact opposite — acceptance. And how wonderful it must feel when you realize that you have been struggling your whole life to be accepted in a mental house, right?

At some point, after studying countless books on communication, empathy, compassion and mutual understanding, or even racism, I came to the conclusion that I would never solve this problem because of a very simple but obvious fact:

Earth is predominately contained, contaminated and controlled by three energy forces or frequencies: Poverty, fear and ignorance. They can all be measured and tested at a vibratory level.

These three energies control the mind and the actions of all humans. And they can't escape them, because their own social system, in the way it is organized, feeds from such common mental state. In other words, their social system blocks the possibility of any evolution.

At the same time, humans cannot see that, that the salvation they seek comes in the form of people like me, whom they hate deeply. For my light, reveals all of their darkness, and the most avoided fears. And they then typically say that I am very negative, not realizing I awake all the negativity within them by making them confront it.

These three frequencies seem simple to understand, reason why the rich are so admired. They seem to have transposed them within the physical world. And that is so, to a certain extent. For you see, neither the ones who admire them and wish to become wealthy, or the wealthy themselves, know that the laws of reincarnation will drive them towards poverty again, through the cyclic laws of karma and fortune. Whatever goes up must come down, and whatever goes down must come up.

In a sense, just as the wealthy are the ones who give the most to charity, charities will always be needed for as long as we have poverty. And the poor, even if once rich, in a previous lifetime, may find themselves needing the wealth and support of the wealthy in another.

The only way to break free from this system of things, from this rollercoaster of excess and nothingness, emotional abundance and its opposite — suffering, is by leveling the planet under one law of equality. And again, we come to the concept of collective consciousness, for you can't consider it until you consider empathy and understanding for all beings on Earth and the reincarnation cycles they expose themselves to in every lifetime. Obviously, that would eliminate both arrogance and victimization within you. It would make you a more wise and empathic person. And that's why both states of mind are so important.

COLLECTIVE CONSCIOUSNESS

On the other hand, too many people erroneously believe, due to their low frequency and the low frequency of the majority, which is controlled by those three elements I mentioned above, that if more is stolen from the rich, if communism prevails on all planet, somehow, their life will become better; and this idea is completely wrong, even catastrophic, despite the fact that the world gets poorer and may one day lead exactly towards this end.

The solution is the opposite, as in embracing capitalism as a form of self-awareness and self-sustenance, and this comes in the form of Entrepreneurship. This is the only way to eradicate poverty from Earth. And this conclusion is easy to make, once we look at the real cause behind these three frequencies, for they are not what they seem but manifestations of certain paradigms being fed by the collective on the planet.

How are Humans Controlled by Their Vibrations?

Fear manifests itself within a competitive mindset, the idea that for some to have others must have not, and it's an idea of scarcity, which manifests itself in the promotion of hierarchic values, deprived from compassion and empathy.

Fear makes people selfish, manipulative and stuck within their brain and their need to control others, to lie, to deceive and to take advantage of others, as if they were just objects. Fear drives people downwards, towards terror, narcissism and emotional abuse. Fear makes people unemphatic and psychotic. It is the lowest frequency, and the opposite of love, which is the highest.

Ignorance is usually misunderstood by people of earth, because they tend to confuse it with arrogance. Most people attribute intelligence to popular authors they read and the things they know and the diplomas they have, or how meaningful is the college degree they possess. But that type of intelligence is deceptive and traps the mind within more paradigms — the paradigms created by others, and that enslave the mind within the same values that keep society formed as found.

In other words, this type of intelligence is not intelligence, but the regurgitation and repetition of values between generations to keep wealth within the same few, and deny evolution — a true spiritual transformation of the soul — to the many.

This type of education makes people arrogant and even more stupid, because they end up denying change more fiercely, and becoming more self-absorbed within their ideals, which they can't see and don't want to see, that have been imposed by others. It is then no coincidence that the academia promotes communism as the ideal system, for that is the system of the masses, that is poverty being kept within the masses. And that is also why so many people with college degrees can't find a job, change their life or create a business. They are very stupid in a very unique way; their head is typically found full of useless knowledge and self-destructive social ideologies.

Poverty also has its own frequency; it's the opposite of wealth. But few know what poverty really is, even though many books have shown us somehow the direction out of this mindset.

Poverty is often confused by many with visual things, just as wealth. They compare the poor with the rich, in material possessions. And well, many people think that I am poor, precisely for this reason. They ignore that I tend to always make other people much richer than me. And the reason why, is that with the exact same values, you can have whatever you want and in the quantity you want, and that is exactly what wealth it.

Now, it doesn't fit the mind of the many, to think that I don't want more money. And I can't say I don't want either. But my priority in life is not money, but my books. I do have businesses, and I attract income from different sources, and I know many techniques to attract wealth; but I also struggle with my limiting human energy, and the huge amount of energy I must channel to my work.

From morning to night, Monday to Sunday, all I do is write, write, and write. I don't really have much time to socialize, to cook, to even apply what I write about. I just write, write and write, from the moment I wake up until I go to sleep.

My days consist, literally, in leaving my apartment early morning, have my breakfast outside, and then work the whole day until the place where I am has to close, and I can't continue anymore. Sometimes I do continue my work at home, but more often than not, I am so exhausted that as soon as I arrive home, I fall asleep. And this is how my life has been since I started writing books.

Obviously, I have done many other things before, but I also quickly had to stop them due to lack of time. I can't write so many books, about so many things, and still do many other things. It's impossible. And the real world, well, this real world, of disgusting and selfish and very ignorant human creatures, doesn't give me many more options in order to do more with my time. And I really hate to waste it on people without empathy or relationships that go around and around their own dramas, simply because people are obsessed with their own theaters and only see in these dramatizations a way to fulfill themselves and feel alive.

Why do People Create Drama?

Almost the totality of the human race is completely insane, and that's why, like the schizophrenics on a mental hospital, they keep dramatizing their own stories, using others as pawns and objects to fulfill their needs. They think that they need other people but that's a complete lie. They use one another, to fulfill egotistical and irrational needs, projected unto them by their own decadent and insane soul. And for me, the mental pressure of such insanity is so huge, that I can't deal with most of the things people claim to be normal. Because they will never feel normal to me. Quite often, such emotional states that people call normal, damage my capacity to write and think effectively. And it's because I feel things so organically, that anger can literally make me go into a meltdown of emotional suffering for several days, even weeks.

Almost the entirety of the planet never truly lives. From birth to death, humans insist on drama after drama after drama. They have no idea of what life is. And I can see it in their face.

As a matter of fact, the more arrogant a human is, the more psychotic such person will be. Because that is what arrogance is; it's the dramatization of a very profound state of psychosis, as a deep sleep, a dream, or more simply, a form of death.

Most humans are not truly alive but representing their own mental dramas. And they are so obsessed with their dramas that they will attack you if you try to wake them up.

They often congregate around others who want to represent their dramas, people who have similar dramas, or that are willing to play the roles they seek for their own imaginary movie of what life is; and to say that people are just playing out their dreams is to be too nice about them, for they are literally insane.

Earth is literally an asylum. If you haven't or can't see that, you are still as crazy as anyone else.

This analysis can be compared with the paradox of the fish underwater: How can you know that you are underwater before someone catches you out of the water? And how can you know what water is, unless you face the possibility of death?

This is why death is so scary for human beings: It represents being caught out of water.

The Relation Between Wealth and Mental Health

Now, what does wealth have anything to do with mental health? Well, I also, personally, did not know this, until I realized that the only way you will ever be a successful entrepreneur, is if you do things that others consider crazy, irrational, out of the system, or even illegal and impossible.

Isn't it interesting that the only way you will ever be free from the asylum called Earth, is if you act differently from the insane, while they themselves call you crazy? It's really interesting to see things from this perspective, but there's no better metaphor I know for what I want you to see.

As you improve your capacity to reason better, to think independently, and more rationally, as you acquire more knowledge about how the world works — its strengths and weaknesses, you will inevitably learn how to take advantage of what you possess in wisdom, and money will be attracted to you in the form you desire for yourself. And so, it is no surprise that the wealthy all share the same values, and all of them tend to have few, if any, friends. Most of them hate and despise the majority, and see poverty as a sickness, not a financial condition. And now you can see why thanks to this book.

Poverty is indeed a mental disease, with its own frequency, as any other disease. And as Jim Rohn said, "Being broke is bad, but being stupid is what's really bad. And what's really, really bad is being broke and stupid. Nothing's much worse than that! Unless you're sick. Sick, broke and stupid, that's about as far as you can fall unless you're ugly. Surely that would be the ultimate; ugly, sick, broke and stupid."

Indeed, those are the worse conditions; and the poor tend to attract them all, and not just one. The poor often feel miserable, are always afraid to lose their money and job, have many friends they hate or hate them, are envious, and basically, live in a perpetual hell of ultra decadence.

Now, what is the opposite of this? The opposite is, obviously, love and faith. And whenever I meet someone asking me how to be rich, this is what I teach. Those who can see it and apply, become rich very fast. Those who can't, continue poor.

I've made many people become far much wealthier than me, by simply asking them what they love to do, helping them organize that into a business idea that is applicable, and then showing them that with faith they could make it work. And all of them, or at least the ones who had faith in themselves, were able to, after a few months, become rich and quit their job.

Now, in what regards the people who think I am not rich enough to give advise about money, I must say this: If I do not work, I can still pay a rent, pay for food, and live in any country I want. That is what I always wanted. I am not jealous of the rich that can't stop. But I do admire those who work to make more and can stop whenever they want. And that's the group where I want to belong.

Now, how to get there is another story. For as a writer, I have to work with the tools given to me. This is my first passion, and it's what I do the most. And yet, isn't interesting that I attract all the information present in my books? Or that nearly all my books became bestsellers in multiple platforms?

One could question how is it possible that I can write so much, while not seeing how my advice on money comes in the same form. Again, this is why poverty and wealth have a frequency: This frequency is creativity.

The Greatest Secret to Wealth and Abundance

If you can attract ideas that benefit you and others, you are wealthy. This is why typically, rich families promote art. Art is wealth. Aesthetics is wealth. And the wealthy like to paint, write books, play music, dance, and do other activities that are related to an expanding of the creative mindset that connects them to the divine source of all information, of all that ever was and ever will be.

God is in the past and in the future, and so, the wealthy are lovers of art, because, as Plato claimed, art connects us to God at all levels: "Beholding beauty with the eye of the mind, he will be enabled to bring forth, not images of beauty, but realities, and bringing forth and nourishing true virtue to become the friend of God and be immortal, if mortal man may"; "Music is a moral law. It gives soul to the universe, wings to the mind, flight to the imagination, and charm and gaiety to life and to everything"; "Poets utter great and wise things which they themselves do not understand."

The more you explore your talents within you, by playing an instrument, painting or training yourself in any other artistic activity you love to do, the more you connect yourself to this source we call God, and by definition, the more ideas you attract to your life.

These ideas will come according to the vision you hold in your mind. And so, you will always have more abundance in correspondence to your thoughts.

In my case, such ideas and thoughts come in the form of knowledge. I constantly receive them in my dreams, during my writing, and basically, all the time throughout the day. I can channel spirits from Earth, extraterrestrials and more. I have telepathic abilities and many others, that grant me the capacity to access knowledge in a huge variety of ways, most of which are very scary for most people, reason why I shall never reveal. But I can literally tap into the past and the future, and travel in time with my mind as well. And this is why my books have such a power that readers claim to never have found in any other famous author, from the present or the past.

I am, indeed, changing the world, as I always wanted, because of all the mental powers I have to do so, but I was also born for this. I am on Earth to reveal this information to the rest of mankind. And the more I do it, the more my memories on other planets are revealed to me, the more my capacities to access any form of information increase, and at the same time, the more I am hated by a whole planet that vibrates at a much lower frequency than mine.

This, because, truly, creativity is the highest frequency possible for a human body on Earth — it merges the ability to postulate, dream and imagine at the same time. And most human beings are found in the opposite of this spectrum — in a state of self-delusion.

All religions of Earth should be worshipping creative thoughts and following guidance towards this direction, in order to truly promote spirituality and ascension, but ironically, if such was the case, they would have no followers.

This known, I personally endure the contrasts of ignorance and blindness with the light I bring to the world, by focusing on my freedom instead.

And how much money do you need to be free? Not much, as a matter of fact; and that's why I feel that my wealth is being blocked by myself only, for if I keep exercising my own mind to go beyond these concepts, so that I can make more money, travel more, and expand my freedom also more, I will. And yet, by the same laws that govern Earth, this will only happen within a perfect balance, and in which more humans are accepting my knowledge, applying it, and transforming the very planet where I step my feet every day.

How to Transcend Mass Consciousness

If you wish me to be more technical about everything I wrote here, know the following: The fear frequency is one of the lowest, alongside with guilt and shame. Its opposite is joy, happiness and love — the love for what you want, for your dreams, for what you like to do, and for what you want to do.

If you want to experience love, you must live love, by making decisions that are in line with your desires, even if you regret them later in time, or they may not work as expected.

Do not have vacations once a year, but live where you feel that you are on vacations all the time. And transform what you love to do into your full-time job, or work towards making it possible.

Don't waste your time in surrounding yourself with people you don't truly like, appreciate or admire, just because they are members of your family or long term friends, but learn to confront others with a higher self-esteem, and by telling them which changes you demand from them, while making an ultimatum that, if they refuse that, you will leave them.

I have done this with my own family and I have no regrets even though they see me as evil. I told them that without respect and honesty they would never see me again. They kept insulting me and lying, and so I literally stopped talking to all.

I have done the same with all my relationships. I do not tolerate anyone who can't respect my work, and personality, who doesn't admire me and show that admiration. It is and should be seen by everyone as a minimum prerequisite to any association, but sadly, most people ignore these basic values, because they also have no self-love or self-esteem.

That's why they suffer and will always suffer for as long as they refuse to learn about love in its basic form, instead of seeking for love outside themselves. Self-love is the basis of a higher frequency state.

As for the frequency of ignorance, it can easily be changed with more understanding and empathy, and this comes in the form of a consistent reading habit, by learning and assimilating content from a vast variety of sources. And also, can be transformed with the interchange of cultural values, as when one travels the world. But must be found within the greatest contrast or contradictions possible. You should not just learn within one field of knowledge but expand your boundaries beyond what makes you feel comfortable and learn about a vast set of subjects.

As you improve this frequency, you will love knowledge, learn faster, read faster, and improve your awareness.

This habit also raises your chakra level from the physical pleasures and the incessant stream of uncontrollable thoughts, always within your mind, to the highest, in the form of wisdom, enlightenment and more imagination, more beauty and more dreams.

It's the difference between a psychopath stuck within thoughts of self-destruction, of others and oneself, and the opposite — in the form of ideas and imagination and dreams, always flowing to one's mind.

Finally we come to the frequency of wealth, which is basically creativity. You develop this with art, i.e., by learning to play an instrument, painting, whatsoever you wish to paint, drawing, whatsoever you wish to draw, and even dancing, even if you go by yourself to a music festival to enjoy it alone.

It doesn't really matter how you see yourself in this process, as long as you see it as a path of self-discovery, in which the more you do, the more you understand about what makes you happy and what you truly want to do.

Try it all, do it all, and have no boundaries, because art is the best drug for the spirit. If you wish to be high on life all the time, then be it with music and any other form of art. This is the safest way to connect to the divine. And also the fastest way to attract more wealth into your life.

COLLECTIVE CONSCIOUSNESS

Whomsoever teaches poor children to play music, does a great service for mankind. And it's interesting how we often don't notice how important these things are, but they make a huge difference.

It might come as a surprise to you, that the most important subjects in school are typically the most ignored by the majority; but as you can see now, they're art, music and dancing. Parents do more for their daughters and sons by making them learn these things instead of finance or anything else, even though I am not saying that other subjects aren't equally important.

In fact, the beauty of mathematics and even martial arts, is found in their art, when one can see them as art.

Da Vinci demonstrated this perfectly, when bringing the laws of engineering to art and combining them perfectly in his work.

About the Publisher

This book was published by the 22 Lions Bookstore.
For more books like this visit www.22Lions.com.
Join us on social media at:
Fb.com/22Lions;
Twitter.com/22lionsbookshop;
Instagram.com/22lionsbookshop;
Pinterest.com/22LionsBookshop.

www.ingramcontent.com/pod-product-compliance
Lightning Source LLC
Chambersburg PA
CBHW050446010526
44118CB00013B/1707